THE OFI ENGLAND RUGBY ANNUAL 2021

D1631471

England Rugby

A Grange Publication

© 2020. Published by Grange Communications Ltd., Edinburgh, under licence from the Rugby Football Union. The RFU Rose and the words 'England Rugby' are official registered trade marks of the Rugby Football Union.

Printed in the EU.

Photographs © RFU via Getty Images, PA Images and Shutterstock.

ISBN 978-1-913034-94-8

5

CONTENTS

WELCOME, RUGBY FAN!

You're in the right place for the inside story on another amazing year for England Rugby.

We've got loads of great articles, player profiles, activities and amazing pictures just for you. Enjoy!

We began with fond memories of the Rugby World Cup in Japan, and especially England's great victory over New Zealand. Then we saw some crunching performances from both the men's and women's teams in the Guinness Six Nations.

Then coronavirus arrived. Could rugby meet the challenge? Of course it could! Rugby is all about great values and supporting each other when things get difficult. Read on to find out about rugby's response to the crisis.

Rugby – the greatest game in the world. Our game!

2021 GUINNESS SIX NATIONS FIXTURES

ENGLAND V SCOTLAND
Twickenham Stadium, **Saturday 6th February 2021.** Kick-off: 4:45pm

ENGLAND V ITALY
Twickenham Stadium, **Saturday 13th February 2021.** Kick-off: 2:15pm

WALES V ENGLAND
Principality Stadium, Cardiff, **Saturday 27th February 2021.** Kick-off: 4:45pm

ENGLAND V FRANCE
Twickenham Stadium, **Saturday 13th March 2021.**
Kick-off: 4:45pm

IRELAND V ENGLAND
Aviva Stadium, Dublin, **Saturday 20th March 2021.**
Kick-off: 4:45pm

CORONAVIRUS DIARIES

Everything was quite normal until early 2020. And then coronavirus changed... everything. It was the country's worst crisis since the Second World War.
Rugby was cancelled, schools were closed. Thousands of rugby players and fans suddenly had lots of time on their hands.

It was a completely new situation for rugby, and for the country as a whole. Would the game rise to the challenge? Of course it would!

How did the England stars fill their time? How did local clubs respond to the challenge and come to the aid of their communities? Read on and find out...

WE'LL MEET AGAIN...

England

Eddie Jones set the philosophy for his squad: "Rugby has always inspired teamwork. Now, for everyone, it is about how you become a better citizen. One of the values we talk about is togetherness." Eddie himself spent his time keeping fit, communicating by video-conference, sending his players challenges via Twitter and ... walking his dog, Annie.

Fitness

Of course, keeping fit was a major priority for the England players. Jonny May and Vicky Fleetwood were among those sharing their routines with the outside world. It was not easy to keep up with them!

Elsewhere, players burned calories and kept up muscle mass in any way they could – running, exercise bikes, improvised garage gyms, using microwaves for weights (!), press-up challenges – they all got the full treatment.

Boredom

Staying in, missing the friendship and support of their mates was just as hard for the star players as for everyone else. Some, like Mako Vunipola, Henry Slade and Luke Cowan-Dickie spent time practising their video game skills. Others caught up with TV series, painted the house, walked the dog...

Staying Positive... is everything.

As Eddie Jones said in April 2020: "I think it's important for everyone to keep safe, keep well, keep positive and be prepared for what's coming because we know we're going to get through this."

EMILY SCARRATT'S INTENSE HOME WORKOUT

SHAUNAGH BROWN'S HOME FITNESS REGIME

CORONAVIRUS DIARIES

COMMUNITY

Rugby clubs are at the heart of their community.

They are places for people to have fun, keep fit, make life-long friends and help others. Not to mention playing some rugby as well!

The World Turned Upside Down
Coronavirus changed our lives completely. People needed each other more than ever before. Would rugby clubs step up to the plate and help keep the country running? You bet they would!

Here are just a few examples from rugby clubs up and down the country.

ENGLAND

Tabard RFC delivered thousands of meals to disadvantaged children in their local area.

Winchester RFC provided facilities for their local blood donation service.

Grimsby RUFC donated their boot bags to the local hospital. Now the medical staff had somewhere to keep their respirators!

Beaconsfield RFC delivered hundreds of prescriptions to home addresses.

Vulnerable people were able to stay at home and avoid the risk of infection.

Of course, HQ was not left out of the picture. As well as the pitch being decorated with the NHS logo, the famous Twickenham stadium was also transformed into one of the country's first drive-through coronavirus testing centres.

Thank you rugby! Thank you to all who contributed to our sport's amazing effort! We are all proud to be involved in such a great game.

2020 GUINNESS SIX NATIONS

Top of the table, a Triple Crown in the bag and a series of good performances after a disappointing start. This was the report on England after four games of the championship.

What everyone would remember, of course, was that it was the season interrupted by coronavirus. All England could do was wait until it was safe, and then play their remaining match, against Italy.

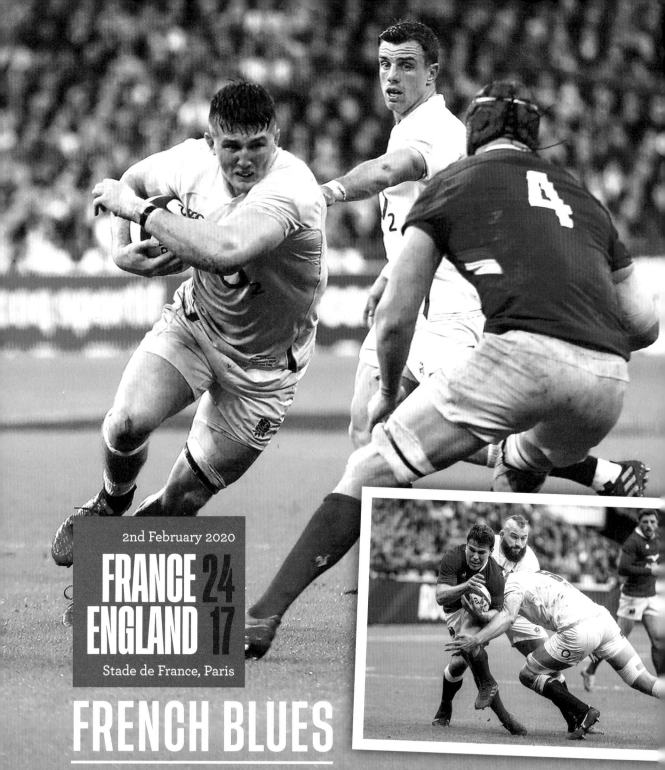

2nd February 2020

FRANCE 24
ENGLAND 17

Stade de France, Paris

FRENCH BLUES

A slightly disappointing performance from England allowed France to register a narrow win.

Jonny May provided the highlight of the afternoon from England's point of view. His two magnificent second-half tries contributed to his scoring an incredible six tries in three games against the French.

Jonny was a keen schoolboy soccer player, and he showed his ability when he side-footed his own kick over the line for his first try. Soon afterwards, he received the ball just inside the French half and tight

to the touchline. Seven seconds later he was touching down near the posts, having run nearly 50 metres and left the defence trailing.

Unfortunately, it was too little, too late for England. France, inspired by the superb Antoine Dupont, scored three tries and managed to hold on for the victory, despite England's late pressure.

The first round also saw victories for Ireland and Wales.

MOMENT OF THE MATCH
Jonny turns on the afterburners for his second try. Wow!

14

STORM MURRAYFIELD

Talk about bad weather! England beat Scotland in a tight game, with both teams battling incredible wind and rain.

A massive storm broke over Murrayfield as the players entered the pitch, and the conditions dominated the game. Kicks were blown backwards and the rain sometimes blinded the players. This was definitely not the time for running rugby!

England had not beaten Scotland since 2017, and were very pleased to regain the magnificent Calcutta Cup. It was an occasion for solid defence, and England were lucky to have players like Sam Underhill and Maro Itoje. They tackled everything that moved and slowly got the upper hand over a brave Scotland team.

England's replacements were crucial. They looked stronger and more dynamic than their Scottish equivalents. Substitute Ellis Genge sealed the game with a powerful drive to score in the 69th minute.

With Owen Farrell also scoring a conversion and two penalties, England won 13-6. Elsewhere Ireland beat Wales, and France defeated Italy.

MOMENT OF THE MATCH

Hang on a minute! Prop Ellis Genge has to hold the ball in place as Owen Farrell lines up a kick.

23rd February 2020

ENGLAND 24
IRELAND 12

Twickenham Stadium,
London

ENGLAND LAY DOWN THE LAWES

England's best performance since their World Cup semi-final triumph over New Zealand!

Ireland had no answer as a pumped-up England showed their class. The gap between the two teams was much bigger than the scoreline would suggest.

Courtney Lawes was voted man of the match, but the award could easily have gone to many of his team mates. The front row were superb, as was Maro Itoje. The backs, too, dominated their Irish opponents.

England's three tries came from George Ford, Elliot Daly and Luke Cowan-Dickie. Owen Farrell converted all three tries and added a penalty as well.

England were aggressive but disciplined, controlling the game with great tactical awareness. Skill levels were superb throughout the team.

Coach Eddie Jones was delighted with England's performance, even cheekily saying that if it was a cricket match he would have declared at half time.

France were top of the table after their victory over Wales and Scotland beat Italy.

MOMENT OF THE MATCH
Manu Tuilagi's early charge shows Ireland what they are in for. Would you like to stop him?

STRANGE DAYS

There was a slightly strange atmosphere inside Twickenham as England comfortably beat Wales to win the Triple Crown.

Prime Minister Boris Johnson was in the crowd for England's last match before the coronavirus lockdown. The virus was already dominating the headlines, but England were fully focused on the game. A tremendous start saw England score within five minutes: Anthony Watson crossing the line after a brilliant lineout move.

England against Wales is always a fiercely fought match. This was no exception, and Wales were never going to give in against a determined England team. However, a try from Elliot Davy and accurate kicking saw England 20-9 up at half time.

The match was effectively won by Manu Tuilagi's 61st minute try, although his indiscipline and high tackle cost England as he was shown a red card.

7th March 2020

ENGLAND 33
WALES 30

Twickenham Stadium, London

MOMENT OF THE MATCH

Ben Young's sublime inside pass confuses the entire Welsh team, and puts Anthony Watson through for his try. Sweet as a nut!

PROFILE

TOM CURRY

THE SLEEPWALKING KAMIKAZE KID

You probably know Tom Curry as one of the best rugby players in the world. Tom has an incredible work-rate and amazing speed and power. He is everywhere on the pitch!

You probably also know that he has a twin brother, Ben. They play together for Sale Sharks, and many people think they will one day appear in the same England team.

You definitely know he was one of England's stars at RWC 2019. Tom played every minute of the campaign, and was simply brilliant against New Zealand.

But did you know he has a reputation as an eccentric in the England camp?
Why? Well, he is known as a sleepwalker who occasionally tackles televisions!
His teammates enjoy his unique style of conversation, but are not so keen on his snoring.

Did you know that he had a trial for Manchester City? How about the fact that he scored on his Premiership debut? Was man of the match on his England debut? That he was one of the youngest England players ever?

There is lots to learn about this amazing player. But don't worry, he looks set to be an England star for years to come. You have lots of time to get to know him.

THE GREATEST PERFORMANCE EVER?

Who can forget England's magnificent performance in the 2019 Rugby World Cup semi-final?

England beat New Zealand 19-7, but in truth it was never that close. England simply blew New Zealand away with passion and power.

Was this England's best performance ever? Well, maybe - but here are some other great matches you might not be so familiar with.

1936

Prince Alexander Obolensky scored two wonder tries as England beat the All Blacks for the first time in history. Obolensky's pace and daring is still remembered more than 80 years later.

ENGLAND 13
NEW ZEALAND 0

ENGLAND 20
AUSTRALIA 17

2003

RUGBY WORLD CUP FINAL

The only time England have landed the ultimate prize in rugby. Everyone remembers Jonny Wilkinson's drop goal to win the match in the last minute of extra time, it was really the ultimatee team effort.

2001

OK, Romania weren't the strongest team in the world. But scoring 20 tries still takes some doing! The Twickenham scoreboard couldn't keep up – it could only go up to 99!

ENGLAND 134
ROMANIA 0

2003

If you want to be the best, then you have to beat the best. Just before the 2003 Rugby World Cup, England went on a tour to Australia and New Zealand, and beat both of them. A massive psychological advantage before the world tournament's first whistle was even blown.

ENGLAND 15
NEW ZEALAND 13

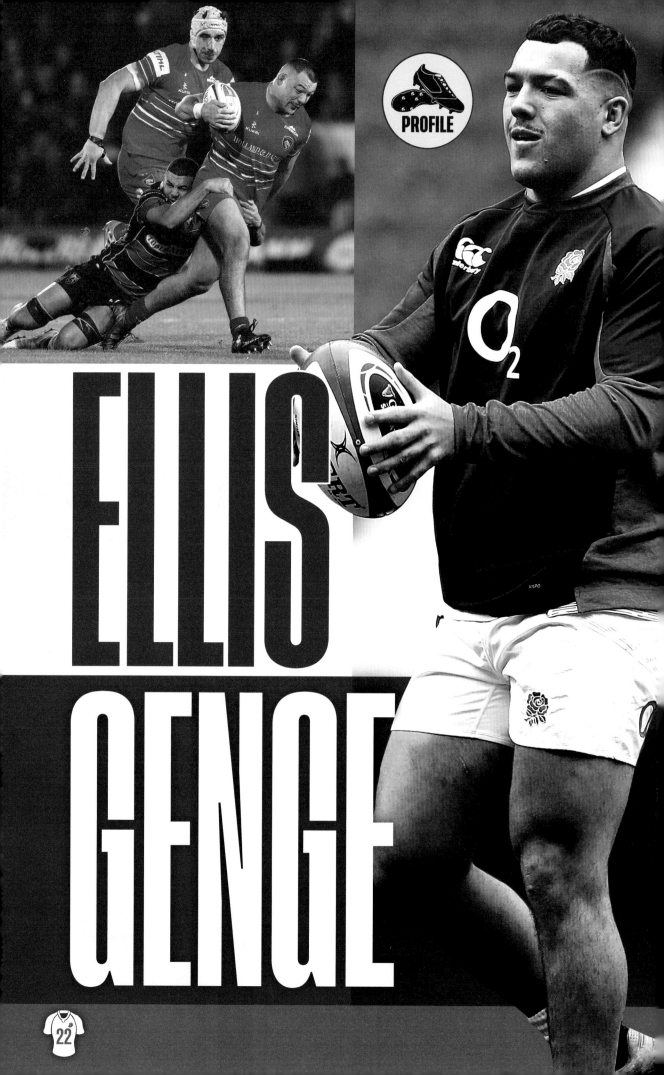

ELLIS GENGE

22

He's got the power!

Ellis Genge loves the physical side of rugby. He is famous for his rampaging runs, knocking potential tacklers out of the way like nine-pins. Not many opponents relish facing his power and aggression!

Ellis helped win a tight game against Scotland in last year's Six Nations. First, with the scores tied, he helped a rock-solid England pack win a late scrum. Then, sniffing an opportunity, he was quickly up and ready at the edge of a ruck close to the Scottish line. With Maro Itoje and Kyle Sinckler at his side, no one was going to stop him going over!

Game won!

Ellis admits that early in his career he could be volatile on the pitch, and give away silly penalties. He has learnt to control his aggression - without losing the edge that makes him such a dangerous opponent.
Off the pitch, Ellis is determined to show that rugby is a game for everyone – that it's not important where you come from or what school you went to. What matters is what you can do on the pitch.

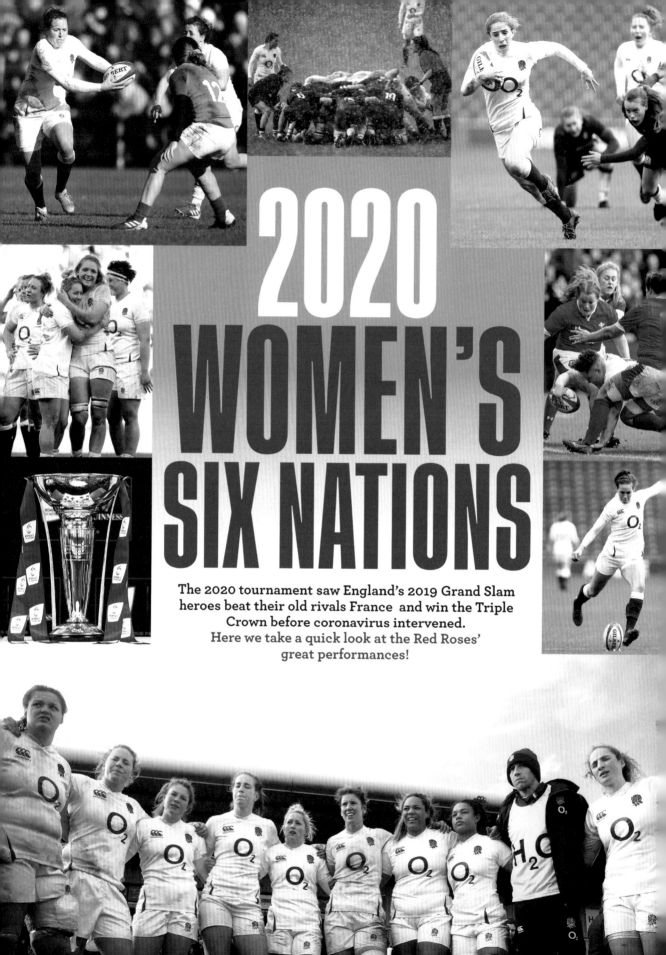

2020 WOMEN'S SIX NATIONS

The 2020 tournament saw England's 2019 Grand Slam heroes beat their old rivals France and win the Triple Crown before coronavirus intervened.
Here we take a quick look at the Red Roses' great performances!

24

FRANCE 13
ENGLAND 19

France have been England's main rivals recently, and were playing at home in the first match of the tournament. Emily Scarratt sealed a tight victory with a try in the 61st minute. Job done!

A strong Ireland side were effectively beaten inside 30 minutes as England crossed the line for three early tries. Two more were added later on.

ENGLAND 27
IRELAND 0

SCOTLAND 0
ENGLAND 53

The match was delayed by Storm Ciara, and moved from Glasgow to an empty Murrayfield Stadium. England's players weren't bothered by the delay or by a blizzard during the match. They scored eight tries in a comfortable victory. The match saw Emily Scarratt become England's highest-ever points scorer.

Wow! England demolished Wales in the last game before the tournament was postponed. Poppy Cleall was almost unstoppable, running in three as England scored a total of ten tries.

ENGLAND 66
WALES 0

WORDSEARCH

Can you find the 20 words related to the England women's rugby team in the maze of letters? Look carefully – they might be vertical, diagonal or even back-to-front! Happy hunting! Answers on page 60

```
M  F  V  M  R  Z  Y  R  T  N  R  U  C  K  L
R  C  T  S  R  E  B  R  E  A  C  H  M  R  Z
B  S  K  C  A  R  F  K  Z  C  C  H  Y  N  G
F  F  S  E  P  D  Z  E  Z  X  F  D  L  N  J
L  J  N  A  N  L  I  P  R  O  X  L  L  L  V
E  N  A  J  P  N  P  D  R  E  A  N  S  I  T
E  L  I  B  R  Z  A  W  A  E  E  E  C  N  T
T  H  R  A  X  B  A  H  L  R  S  T  I  T  A
W  K  A  C  P  R  V  C  K  O  O  A  T  L  R
O  I  B  K  D  F  Y  K  R  R  T  R  T  N  A
O  C  R  S  V  P  C  D  Y  P  R  Q  E  B  C
D  K  A  T  P  K  E  V  A  L  V  R  K  V  S
P  O  B  O  X  R  B  C  C  N  M  P  C  T  J
J  F  P  N  O  T  E  L  D  D  I  M  E  Q  G
G  F  S  A  R  A  H  B  E  R  N  N  B  C  K
```

Adidas	Forwards	Referee
Backs	KickOff	Ruck
Barbarians	McKenna	SarahBern
Beckett	Middleton	Scaratt
Breach	Pass	Try
Captain	PoppyCleall	Victory
Fleetwood	RedRoses	

ON THE ROAD

This year England (and thousands of their fans) will travel to the magnificent Principality Stadium in Cardiff.

England have been playing in Wales since 1882, but the Millennium Stadium (as it was then known) was only opened for the 1999 Rugby World Cup.

The Principality is famous for its retractable roof and the fantastic atmosphere generated by the Welsh fans. England fans, however, are often heard loud and proud at the stadium. The team has done well, winning six of the 13 games they have played there. England even have a positive points difference at the ground, 254 points to 228!

By contrast, older England fans will remember a painful period in the 1970s and '80s. Superb Welsh teams prevented a single English victory in Cardiff for 28 years!

England now have plenty of their own great players, and they will be looking for victory in this year's match.

PRINCIPALITY STADIUM

TWICKENHAM STADIUM

PRINCIPALITY BUILDING SOCIETY	PRINCIPAL PARTNER	BRITISH AIRWAYS
CARDIFF, WALES	LOCATION	TWICKENHAM, LONDON
1999	FIRST INTERNATIONAL	1910
74,500	CAPACITY	82,000

ENGLAND GREATS

JASON LEONARD

Jason Leonard is one of England rugby's all-time greats. Here are just some of the amazing facts about this true rugby legend.

• **Jason is England's most capped men's player ever! ***

• He played 114 times for his country.

• **He was very accident-prone as a child, apparently being run over six times!**

• Jason loves the social side of rugby and his nickname is 'The Fun Bus'.

• **He is the only English player to play in two Rugby World Cup finals – in 1991 and 2003.**

• He was badly injured in 1992, and played for 11 years with a bone graft in his neck.

• **As well as winning the RWC in 2003, Jason won four Grand Slams with England.**

• A proud East Londoner, Jason started his career with Barking RFC. He now works hard to encourage people from all backgrounds to get involved in rugby.

• **Jason toured three times with the British Lions.**

• Jason has been the President of the Rugby Football Union and is now Chairman of the British and Irish Lions.

• **He played internationally as both tight and loose-head prop.**

• He was awarded an OBE in 2004.

*England's all-time most capped player is Rochelle 'Rocky' Clark. She has 137 caps!

England Rugby

A GAME FOR EVERYONE

Rugby – we all know that it is the best game in the world!

It doesn't matter where you go to school, how good an athlete you are or what happens in your personal life. What's important is that the sport is accessible to you.

Have you told your non-rugby playing friends how good the sport is? Get them involved!

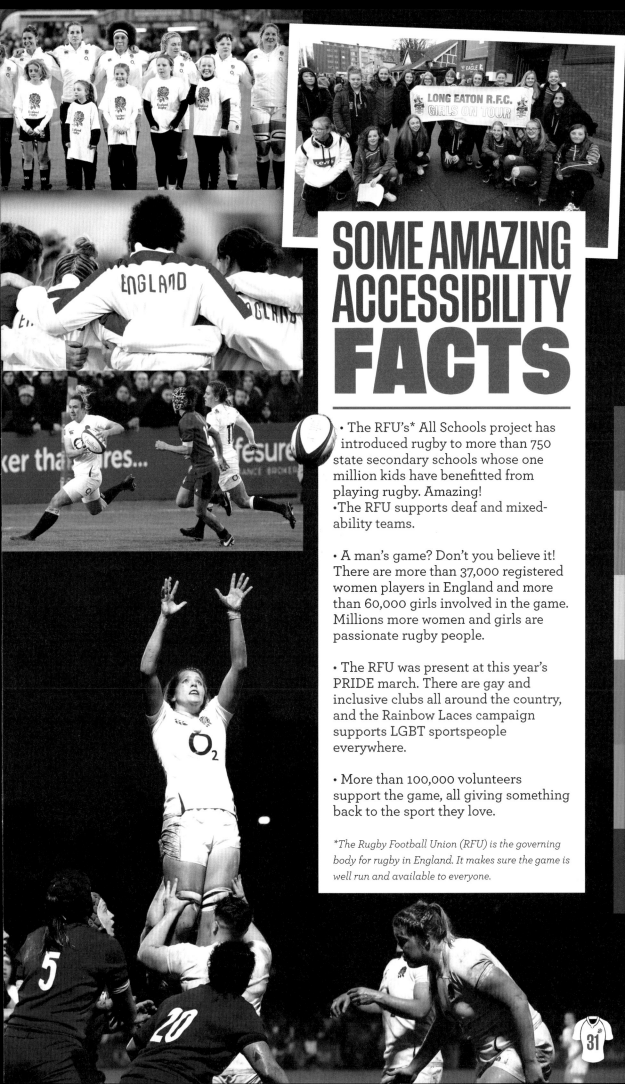

SOME AMAZING ACCESSIBILITY FACTS

• The RFU's* All Schools project has introduced rugby to more than 750 state secondary schools whose one million kids have benefitted from playing rugby. Amazing!

•The RFU supports deaf and mixed-ability teams.

• A man's game? Don't you believe it! There are more than 37,000 registered women players in England and more than 60,000 girls involved in the game. Millions more women and girls are passionate rugby people.

• The RFU was present at this year's PRIDE march. There are gay and inclusive clubs all around the country, and the Rainbow Laces campaign supports LGBT sportspeople everywhere.

• More than 100,000 volunteers support the game, all giving something back to the sport they love.

*The Rugby Football Union (RFU) is the governing body for rugby in England. It makes sure the game is well run and available to everyone.

PLAYER, PITCH, POSITION!

KICKER

Rugby is a game for everyone and rugby players come in all shapes and sizes.

Rugby is also a physical game, and can be technical. While every member of the team needs to be fit and to have good ball-handling skills, each position on the field also has its own requirements and attributes. Some players also accept the extra responsibility of being team captain or goal kicker.

Here's a look at four great players and the skills they need to be world-class in their position or role.

KATY DALEY-MCLEAN

In today's teams, fly halves and full backs accept most of the responsibility for kicking for points. Kicking is a key rugby skill, however, and all players must be comfortable kicking the ball when required.

32

SECOND ROW

MARO ITOJE

Numbers 4 and 5 are the enforcers of the rugby team. They provide monstrous power in the scrum and jump high in the line-out. They are also used to punch holes in the defence and tire opponents out.

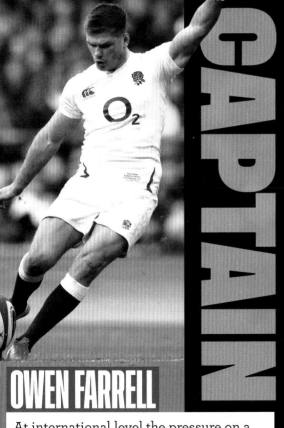

CAPTAIN

OWEN FARRELL

At international level the pressure on a captain is immense. Off the pitch you are ambassador for your team and the sport. During the match you have make crucial, split-second decisions with millions of people watching. Do you fancy it?

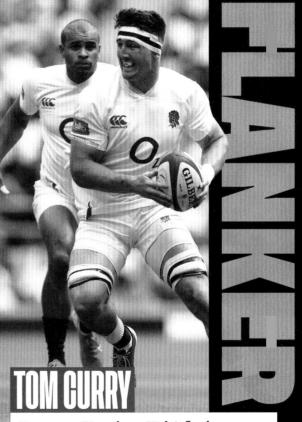

FLANKER

TOM CURRY

Known as 'Kamikaze Kids', flankers (Nos 6 and 7) need great speed and physicality. As well as tackling anything that moves and running powerfully with the ball, a modern flanker also has to be a turnover specialist.

BUILD A PICTURE

Ok, here's a challenge for you. You're going to use your rugby knowledge AND drawing skills to identify a famous rugby figure.

STAGE 1: Match the players to their position. (Clue: the number of the box is SOMETIMES the number the player wears on the pitch). Write player's name AND their letter in the correct box.

STAGE 2: When you have matched all the players, draw the shapes in the correct place in the 'What am I?' box.

Confused? Here's an example.
Box 1 – Prop.   *Hannah Botterman (Letter D) is a prop.*
Write her name and letter in the box.
(Do the other players)
Draw the shape from box D in square 1 of the blank space.

1 Prop	 A Tom Curry
2 Fly Half	B Ben Youngs
3 Second Row	C Jessica Breach
4 Wing	D Hannah Botterman
5 Flanker	E Katy Daly-McLean
6 Full Back	F Manu Tuilagi
7 No. 8	G Elliot Daly
8 Scrum Half	H Maro Itoje
9 Centre	I Sarah Hunter

If you've got them all right you should recognise the figure in the box!

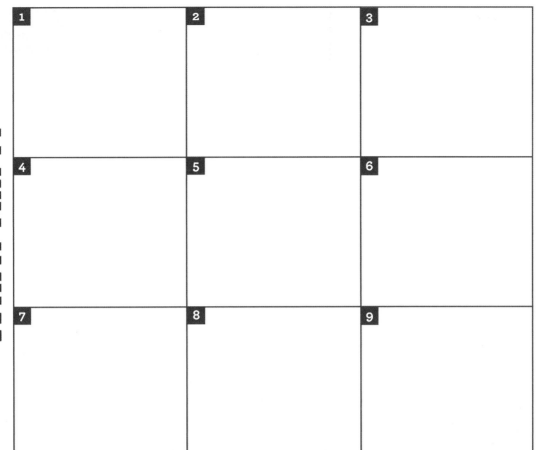

35

EMILY
SCARRATT

36

2019 made it official: Emily Scarratt is the best women's rugby player in the world.

In recognition of her outstanding abilities and achievements in the game, she was awarded the World Rugby Women's 15s Player of the Year title in November 2019.

If you can name it, then Emily has probably done it:
• Women's Rugby World Cup? - Emily scored the winning try as England won the 2014 tournament
• Women's Six Nations? – She has been part of a dominant England side since 2008, winning multiple titles and Grand Slams.
• RPA Women's Players' Player of year? Tick. 2013.
• England's highest-scorer ever? Emily gained this distinction in 2020 as she notched up her 539th point against Scotland.
• Olympic medal? Emily was the captain as Team Britain won bronze in Rio, 2016.

Anything else? Well, she was a rounders international and was offered a professional basketball scholarship when she was just 16!

England women's head coach Simon Middleton summed it up perfectly when he said:

"From a playing point of view, there isn't much that Scaz can't do. I look at her skill-set and it's probably more rounded than any player in the game - male or female.

She can run, pass, kick, catch, high-ball catch, everything... and apart from that she's probably one of the nicest people you could meet."

STATS QUIZ

OK, now it's time for the OFFICIAL RFU stats quiz.
Test your rugby knowledge or simply try your luck.
The answers are on page 61. Good luck!

PUZZLE

1 Which number is NOT worn by a centre?
A 15 B 12 C 13

2 Maro Itoje was England's top tackler at RWC 2019, how many tackles did he make?
A 71 B 14 C 154

3 How many times have England hosted the Rugby World Cup Final?
A 1 B 2 C 3

4 How many matches did England play during the entire 20th Century?
A 9,245 B 243 C 448

5 How many points are awarded for a converted try?
A 3 B 5 C 7

6 Approximately how many rugby clubs are there in England?
A 2,000 B 1,000 C 100

7 With 1,179 points, who is England's all-time record scorer?
A Owen Farrell
B Jonny Wilkinson
C George Ford

8 How many kilometres of toilet paper are used at a capacity match at Twickenham Stadium?
A 500 B 3 C 200

9 True or False? At RWC 2019, Wales (4th place) played more games than England (2nd place).
A True B False

10 What is the capacity of Twickenham Stadium?
A 82,000 B 100,000 C 92,000

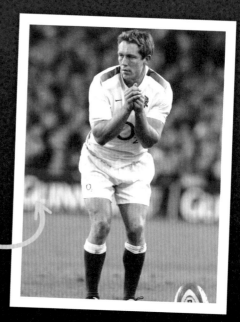

38

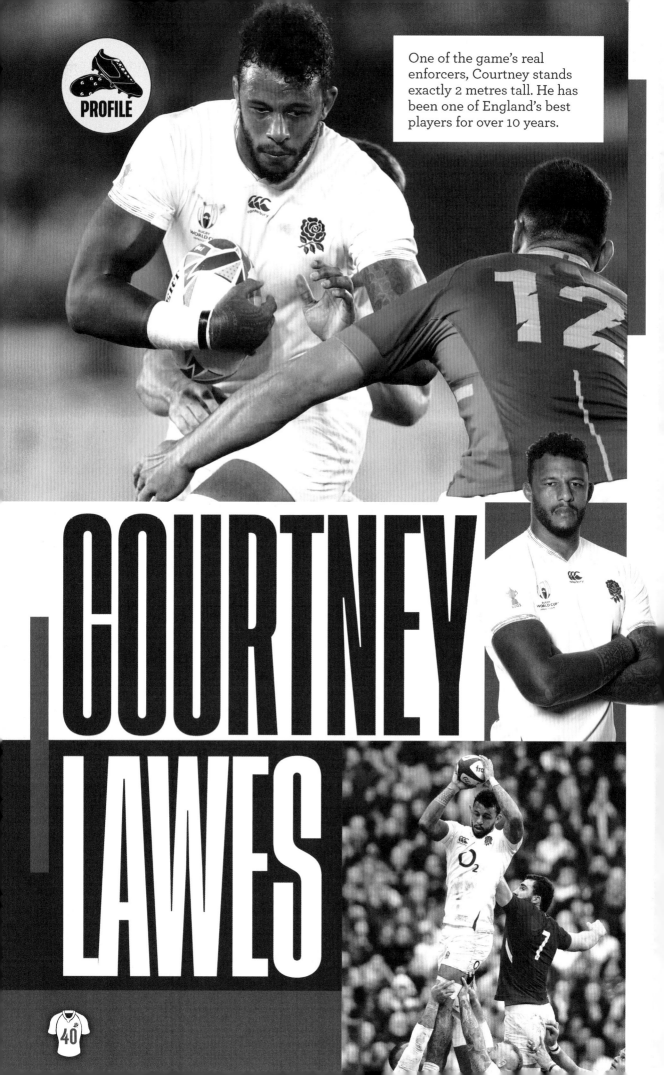

PROFILE

One of the game's real enforcers, Courtney stands exactly 2 metres tall. He has been one of England's best players for over 10 years.

COURTNEY LAWES

40

FACE SWAP

We've got some seriously mixed up players here! But can you tell who they are?

Answers on page 61

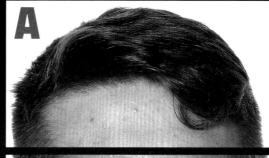

A

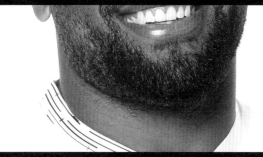

B

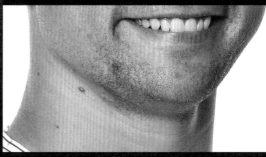

C

SPOT THE BALL

PUZZLE

We've added some extra balls to the picture below.
Can you figure out which one is the right one?

Answer on page 61

42

Hannah has an aunt and an uncle who both played prop for England. There was only ever going to be one game and one position for this powerful player!

HANNAH BOTTERMAN

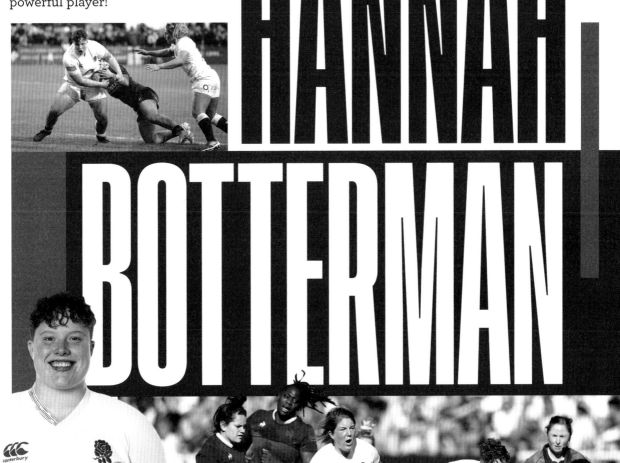

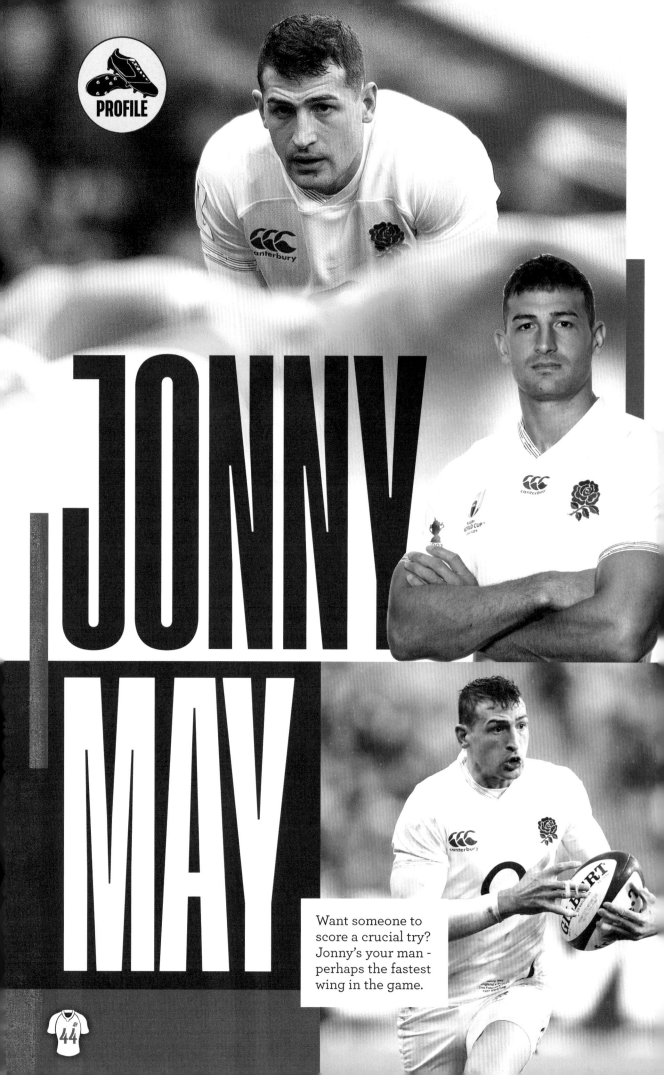

JONNY MAY

Want someone to score a crucial try? Jonny's your man - perhaps the fastest wing in the game.

WORDSEARCH

PUZZLE

Another test of your skill! This time, the words relate more to the men's team. Can you find all 20? Look carefully – they might be vertical, diagonal or even back-to-front! Answers on page 61.

```
G  C  M  A  N  U  T  U  I  L  A  G  I  P  J
U  Y  T  R  E  N  G  L  A  N  D  C  M  U  L
I  A  T  R  L  L  R  H  Y  R  O  S  F  C  B
N  L  N  M  I  K  A  X  X  R  W  H  V  A  S
N  P  N  O  J  P  H  O  O  R  Q  O  B  T  E
E  E  T  A  I  Z  L  N  G  K  X  R  L  T  N
S  R  P  A  M  S  A  E  L  P  V  T  U  U  O
S  A  M  V  C  V  R  T  C  R  O  S  A  C  J
N  K  P  L  I  K  F  E  E  R  M  R  M  L  E
K  C  L  R  M  Y  L  G  V  U  O  G  D  A  I
J  A  U  J  R  C  N  E  R  N  X  W  X  C  D
B  S  K  U  G  I  X  C  M  X  O  W  N  M  D
Q  Q  J  M  W  X  S  P  M  Y  T  C  B  F  E
N  N  M  A  H  N  E  K  C  I  W  T  B  G  T
I  C  F  E  N  I  L  H  C  U  O  T  L  G  N
```

Ball	Guinness	Shorts
CalcuttaCup	Injury	Tackle
Conversion	Japan	Touchline
Coronavirus	ManuTuilagi	TripleCrown
DropGoal	Maul	Twickenham
EddieJones	Replay	Winger
England	Scrum	

45

2019/20 MATCH RESULTS

2019 RUGBY WORLD CUP

22 Sep 2019
ENGLAND **35**
TONGA **3**
Sapporo

26 Sep 2019
ENGLAND **45**
USA **7**
Kobe

5 Oct 2019
ENGLAND **39**
ARGENTINA **10**
Tokyo

19 Oct 2019
ENGLAND **40**
AUSTRLAIA **16**
Oita

46

26 Oct 2019
ENGLAND 19
N. ZEALAND 7
Yokohama

2 Nov 2019
ENGLAND 12
S.AFRICA 32
Yokohama

2020 GUINNESS 6 NATIONS

FRANCE 24-17 ENGLAND

Stade de France, Paris, Sunday 2nd February 2020. Attendance: 79,310

SCOTLAND 6-13 ENGLAND

BT Murrayfield Stadium, Edinburgh, Saturday 8th February 2020. Attendance: 67,144

ENGLAND 24-12 IRELAND

Twickenham Stadium, London, Sunday 23rd February 2020. Attendance: 81,476

ENGLAND 33-30 WALES

Twickenham Stadium, London, Saturday 7th March 2020. Attendance: 81,522

ITALY V ENGLAND

Stadio Olimpico, Rome, Saturday 14th March 2020. MATCH POSTPONED

47

WOMEN'S

England Rugby

49

MEN'S

England Rugby

PLAYER PROFILES

BACKS

ELLIOT DALY

Club	Saracens
Position	Full Back
Height	1.84m
Weight	94kg
Debut	Ireland, 2016
Caps	43
Points	96

OLLIE DEVOTO

Club	Exeter Chiefs
Position	Centre
Height	1.88m
Weight	103kg
Debut	Wales, 2016
Caps	2
Points	-

PLAYER  PROFILES

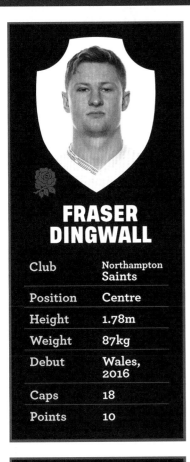

FRASER DINGWALL

Club	Northampton Saints
Position	Centre
Height	1.78m
Weight	87kg
Debut	Wales, 2016
Caps	18
Points	10

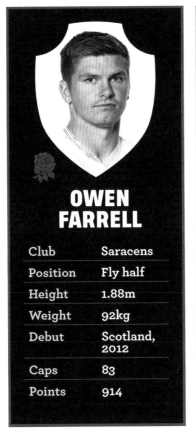

OWEN FARRELL

Club	Saracens
Position	Fly half
Height	1.88m
Weight	92kg
Debut	Scotland, 2012
Caps	83
Points	914

GEORGE FORD

Club	Leicester Tigers
Position	Fly half
Height	1.78m
Weight	84kg
Debut	Wales, 2014
Caps	69
Points	308

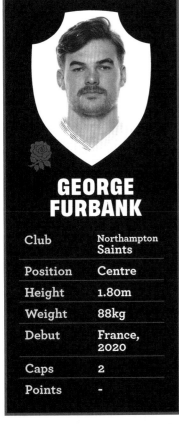

GEORGE FURBANK

Club	Northampton Saints
Position	Centre
Height	1.80m
Weight	88kg
Debut	France, 2020
Caps	2
Points	-

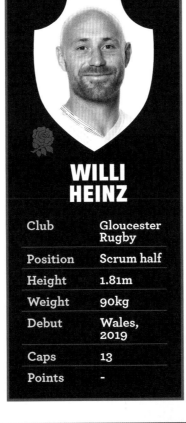

WILLI HEINZ

Club	Gloucester Rugby
Position	Scrum half
Height	1.81m
Weight	90kg
Debut	Wales, 2019
Caps	13
Points	-

BACKS

JOSH HODGE

Club	Newcastle Falcons
Position	Full Back
Height	1.83m
Weight	82kg
Debut	-
Caps	-
Points	-

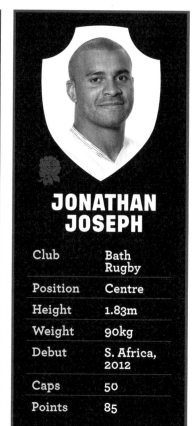

JONATHAN JOSEPH

Club	Bath Rugby
Position	Centre
Height	1.83m
Weight	90kg
Debut	S. Africa, 2012
Caps	50
Points	85

JONNY MAY

Club	Gloucester Rugby
Position	Wing
Height	1.88m
Weight	90kg
Debut	Argentina, 2013
Caps	56
Points	145

ALEX MITCHELL

Club	Northampton Saints
Position	Scrum Half
Height	1.77m
Weight	80kg
Debut	-
Caps	-
Points	-

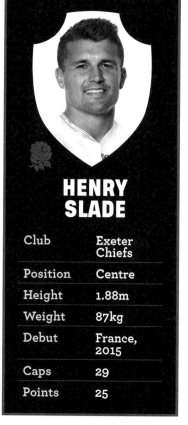

HENRY SLADE

Club	Exeter Chiefs
Position	Centre
Height	1.88m
Weight	87kg
Debut	France, 2015
Caps	29
Points	25

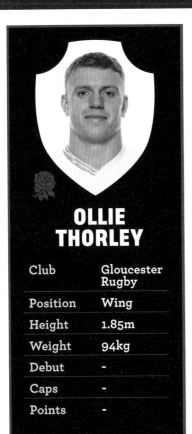

OLLIE THORLEY

Club	Gloucester Rugby
Position	Wing
Height	1.85m
Weight	94kg
Debut	-
Caps	-
Points	-

MANU TUILAGI

Club	Leicester Tigers
Position	Centre
Height	1.85m
Weight	111kg
Debut	Wales, 2011
Caps	43
Points	90

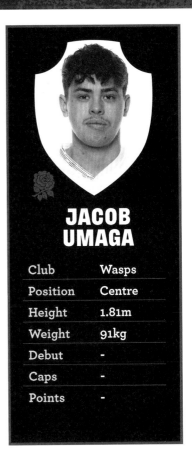

JACOB UMAGA

Club	Wasps
Position	Centre
Height	1.81m
Weight	91kg
Debut	-
Caps	-
Points	-

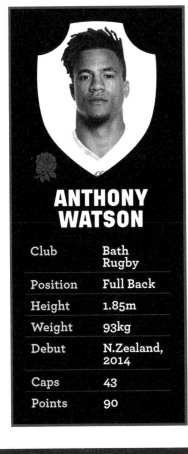

ANTHONY WATSON

Club	Bath Rugby
Position	Full Back
Height	1.85m
Weight	93kg
Debut	N.Zealand, 2014
Caps	43
Points	90

BEN YOUNGS

Club	Leicester Tigers
Position	Scrum half
Height	1.78m
Weight	92kg
Debut	Scotland, 2010
Caps	99
Points	70

Players and statistics correct as of June 2020. England caps and points only.

55

FORWARDS

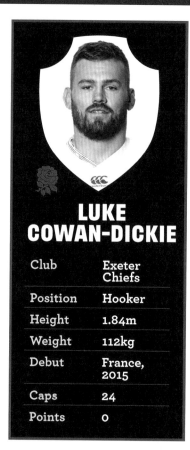

LUKE COWAN-DICKIE

Club	Exeter Chiefs
Position	Hooker
Height	1.84m
Weight	112kg
Debut	France, 2015
Caps	24
Points	0

TOM CURRY

Club	Sale Sharks
Position	Flanker
Height	1.88m
Weight	99kg
Debut	Argentina, 2017
Caps	23
Points	15

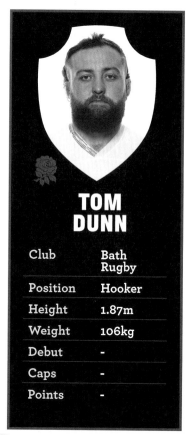

TOM DUNN

Club	Bath Rugby
Position	Hooker
Height	1.87m
Weight	106kg
Debut	-
Caps	-
Points	-

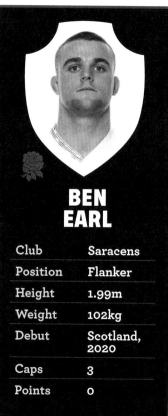

BEN EARL

Club	Saracens
Position	Flanker
Height	1.99m
Weight	102kg
Debut	Scotland, 2020
Caps	3
Points	0

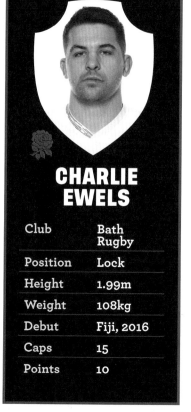

CHARLIE EWELS

Club	Bath Rugby
Position	Lock
Height	1.99m
Weight	108kg
Debut	Fiji, 2016
Caps	15
Points	10

PLAYER 🌹 PROFILES

ELLIS GENGE

Club	Leicester Tigers
Position	Prop
Height	1.87m
Weight	113kg
Debut	Wales, 2016
Caps	18
Points	10

JAMIE GEORGE

Club	Saracens
Position	Hooker
Height	1.83m
Weight	109kg
Debut	France, 2015
Caps	49
Points	15

TED HILL

Club	Worcester Warriors
Position	Flanker
Height	1.95m
Weight	111kg
Debut	Japan, 2018
Caps	1
Points	-

MARO TOJE

Club	Saracens
Position	Lock
Height	1.95m
Weight	115kg
Debut	Italy, 2016
Caps	38
Points	10

GEORGE KRUIS

Club	Saracens
Position	Lock
Height	1.98m
Weight	113kg
Debut	New Zealand, 2014
Caps	45
Points	15

JOE LAUNCHBURY

Club	Wasps
Position	Lock
Height	1.96m
Weight	118kg
Debut	Fiji, 2012
Caps	65
Points	25

Players and statistics correct as of June 2020. England caps and points only.

57

FORWARDS

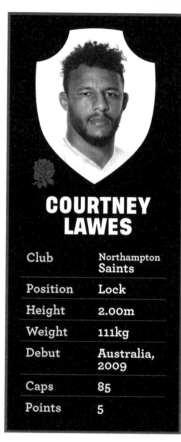

COURTNEY LAWES

Club	Northampton Saints
Position	Lock
Height	2.00m
Weight	111kg
Debut	Australia, 2009
Caps	85
Points	5

LEWIS LUDLAM

Club	Northampton Saints
Position	Flanker
Height	1.88m
Weight	98.5kg
Debut	Scotland, 2019
Caps	8
Points	5

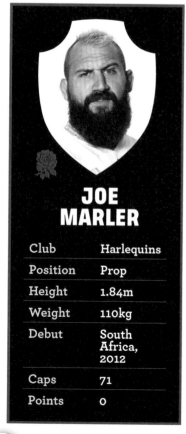

JOE MARLER

Club	Harlequins
Position	Prop
Height	1.84m
Weight	110kg
Debut	South Africa, 2012
Caps	71
Points	0

ALEX MOON

Club	Northampton Saints
Position	Lock
Height	2.01m
Weight	123kg
Debut	-
Caps	-
Points	-

KYLE SINCKLER

Club	Harlequins
Position	Prop
Height	1.83m
Weight	113kg
Debut	South Africa, 2016
Caps	35
Points	5

WILL STUART

Club	Bath Rugby
Position	Prop
Height	1.89m
Weight	124kg
Debut	France, 2020
Caps	3
Points	-

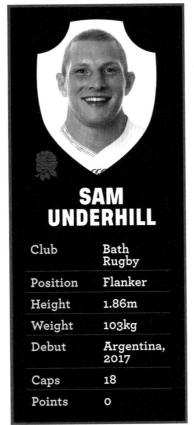

SAM UNDERHILL

Club	Bath Rugby
Position	Flanker
Height	1.86m
Weight	103kg
Debut	Argentina, 2017
Caps	18
Points	0

MAKO VUNIPOLA

Club	Saracens
Position	Prop
Height	1.80m
Weight	121kg
Debut	Fiji, 2012
Caps	59
Points	5

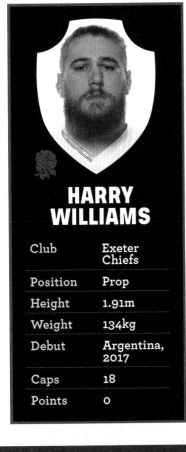

HARRY WILLIAMS

Club	Exeter Chiefs
Position	Prop
Height	1.91m
Weight	134kg
Debut	Argentina, 2017
Caps	18
Points	0

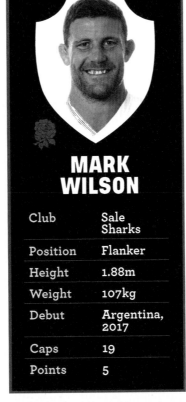

MARK WILSON

Club	Sale Sharks
Position	Flanker
Height	1.88m
Weight	107kg
Debut	Argentina, 2017
Caps	19
Points	5

Players and statistics correct as of June 2020. England caps and points only.

59

QUIZ ANSWERS

PG 26
WORDSEARCH ▶

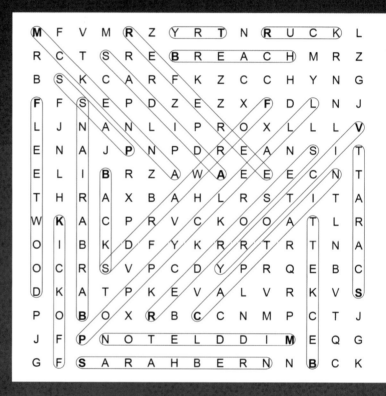

PG 34
BUILD A PICTURE ▶
1D, 2F, 3H, 4C, 5A,
6G, 7I, 8B, 9E

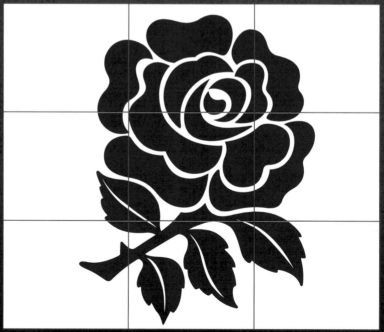

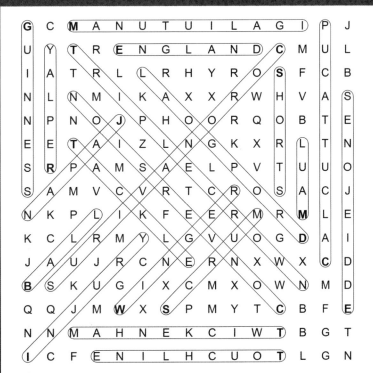

WHERE'S EDDIE JONES?